LEARNING TO SWIM

MARY ROSE CALLAN

bradshaw books
Cork, Ireland

For

Ben, Katie, James and Sean

Acknowledgements

Acknowledgements are due to the editors of the following publications where some of these poems, or versions of them, first appeared: *Boyne Berries 4, Connaught Telegraph, Crannog 14, 16 & 19, Cyphers 62 64 & 66, Dun Laoghaire Rathdown Anthology, The Echoing Years, The Edgeworth Papers IV, Poetry Ireland Review 88 & 95, The Shop 20 & 26, The Stony Thursday Book 5, 6 & 7, The Stinging Fly 25th issue, Thornfield Anthology, the Waterford Review 6, Women's Work VI.*

'Normandy 2004' won the Moore Gold Medal, 'Unseen' won the Clogh Poetry Competition, 'Our Neighbours put in New Windows' was runner-up in the Brendan Kennelly poetry competition.

Thanks to Maire Bradshaw, Nick Sanquest, and the team at Tigh Fili, and to members of the Thornfield Poets writing workshop.

Bradshaw Books gratefully acknowledges the financial assistance of The Arts Council/An Chomhairle Ealaion towards the publication of this volume.

Contents

Part One

Part Two

Part Three

Part 1

Oarsman

One of those
out-of-bounds
river's edge days
of finding
a boat without oars,

you rolled
shirt-sleeves
like whitest skin
over your long
arms stroking

water, your back
close to my knees,
a side face
I struggle to recall,
unlike the boat

sturdy and
burning
white in my heart.

Our Neighbours Put in New Windows

The white van backs into their driveway so quietly,
so early, it could be up to no good

in this cul-de-sac of lost children,
where I lose count

of the frames men are unloading
as easily as I lose count of the days.

The window-ledge I'm leaning on is only good
for one more year, our painter warned -

it's rotting quicker than you think.
Will it be a sudden gust,

glass showering the blanket, or
a clean break, into air, and curtains clamouring?

Fine rain and finer light
sprinkles white frames leaning against the wall,

but they're not ready yet to begin
a lifetime of keeping rain out,

they're like summer girls,
with time on their hands and daydreams glimmering.

The Taste of Lemon

i

Close by, the waiter bones her fish
on a china plate, like a painter
arranging a still-life

of white on white –
say, feathers and sea-shells.
Nothing distracts him,

not even the quiver
in her lover's eyes (he's chosen
the wrong course)

when his steak bleeds,
and she squeezes
cut lemon.

ii

She runs her fingers along granite
where he sliced lemons
with a pocket knife –

it slithers
like the snow when her feet sank
into his footprints,

one, after the other,
though she ached with effort
to match his stride

and catch
distance, slipping between them,
like a gloved hand.

iii
To her left, street-faces harden
like crystals which her lover crushes
with a spoon.

The fog, on her right,
is the city's winter breath. It's bitter
as lemon on her tongue

forcing her to abandon
his eyes in a café watching doors open
on rain,

and embrace swan-light
where the park sleeps like a child
with honey in its hair.

Accident

That morning, thrown over a car,
my nineteen years were dancing

in air, oblivious of the frantic
soundtrack – collective hiss

of the bus queue's
hand-over-mouth. Suddenly

old - two decades spread
like wrinkled clothes

on a still, white sheet - certain
now I'd never see

the dress I was wearing
shrink, or fade

like the silver-blue sparks
before my eyes,

or the bus queue
facing the wrong way.

Learning to Swim

Wrapped all around the headland house
are windows that grow out of glass foundations,

in your fingers the stem of a champagne flute
clear as the sea-pool I float in below

with fish-bones and handfuls of diamond sun,
where my feet cannot touch the ground

where you swallow a mouthful of wine
oblivious of the blue-white cry in my throat, and

I must, there is no other way, I must swim,
and hold on to the splinters of sun on your face.

In Matisse's Chapel

I float on colour between sky and sea
like a long distance swimmer out of breath,

fingers of buttercup on childhood blue,
a loved place brightening

all I remember in a wash of dawn –
that figure, alone, at water's edge

pausing on stone
in the white time of tears

spread like an altar cloth on marble
warmer than wheat.

Swans

Watching her
I become the plump child in ballet class,
my feet going this way and that –

but here women placed near walls in the home
take no notice
though she once held centre stage

like the swan I watched from the disused pier
who came right up to the shallows
where refuse lodged with stones and water-weeds

and thrust her head down, repeatedly,
in charge of her own affairs.
Now she paces in and out of the room,

wearing her coat,
like one who has no intention of staying,
unlike the swan

who later returned to the far side of the lake,
parted the rushes
of her familiar nest. Settled in.

Snow-Woman

She slips her fingers into winter
hedgerows, each time her children offer
potted plants. Invisible under snow,
the brittle twigs can't pierce her skin
or fail to blossom when she enters
a laneway, barefoot, in younger sun,

far from hands that ease her
into a dressing gown. Sheltering
in hedgerows her children cannot see,
she melts in the glare of a red geranium.

Snow-Father

The eldest, shivering in cast-off light
wants him to merge with all the rest,
with a hat like a doorman's
who melts in a backward glance.

Her sister unwinds the scarf she knit
with leftover yarn, sleet hardening
like eyes in the knots. She twists it
around his neck, multicolours
marking him out as her own.

The youngest offers all she can find
in the attic, under the stairs
where the cat sleeps close to the boiler.
His stone eyes wince but she doesn't see
the flicker of snow like an eyelash.

Inside, he's wearing a well cut suit,
shirt, tie, and leather shoes
of diminishing man, his burial
clothes preserved in deep freeze.

Unseen

Two harebells I picked like a thief
when you were shaking sand from your shoes,
mesh in my pocket, making it impossible
to disentangle their stems in that dark
when we overshoot the graveyard
and you say it's too late to turn back.

*

She said she would never rest
with his relatives bones, nor would he
without her. So her eyes, wide-open,
see what the living cannot – twisted
stems, and rifts in a dune
plugged with sand where harebells grew.

*

Out of the blue, our child asks -
Did you visit the grave? You answer for me.
It's late when I unravel drying stems
and bring them to her. She sleeps
with half-closed eyes – harebells
at nightfall, veined with the sea.

*

Someone dressed them in borrowed clothes,
like cut-outs I pasted on cardboard dolls
until paper hooks frayed and they slipped
down the side of the couch – child-fingers
never long enough to grasp
all that disappeared in the threadbare.

Waiting for Rain

i.m. Dorothy Molloy

i. Hare

Like the pulse of – the *Oh*
of first love – it breaks
through leaf-work spinning
midsummer green, teeters
on uncut grass for the second
you're holding your breath,
then off on a white blink
of tail and eye to afternoon

in another time. Pallbearers
lift it, stretched like an H,
from mud. You step back
on trampled grass, stare
at the swollen raincloud
of its belly, swaying
at arms' length, like lost love.

ii. Raincloud

As if a shadow-hand
upended
the sky's basin of hope
leaving a thumbprint
no breath can erase.

iii. Hair's breadth

Mud folds in on itself,
gives nothing away
of the distance between
a stumble at mid night
and spindle
of first steps on grass.

iv. The Comfort of Rain

Leaf
spooning
a rain drop
in the down
spin of rain
is a hare's eye
returning,
the *Oh*
of love. Again

Fine Day

Early afternoon in the brand new
extension, a final
                    touch

of paint. You lean
                    into an alcove
above the cooker, white-

coated like gloss you're applying,
almost disappearing,

thin, tall, in your prime.

I offer words about this fine
day, half-hearted, spattering
                            silent

brushstrokes, over-shoulder smile.
Before another
                    full day
                            passes,

hurrying to meet a friend,
your breath, your heart's beat

all at once
            ceases

in a future we can't imagine in this
room, a new space of lost light

reclaimed from the garden.

African Bride
for Nosianai

Months crossing
the continent
by four-wheel drive,
camel and mule train,
takes them to
this part of her story –

takes it to me. Her face
in close-up
on the journal's page,
a single tear
hollowed
between nose and cheekbone.

When I cover it
with my finger
she's no longer a bride
waiting,
eyes closed,

while a path is cleared
of branch and leaf
to her unknown
husband's home,
listening

to the warning
not to look back,
her father's blessing
of milk
on her head and breasts,

she's a child,
lost in sleep,
cold
as the stone tear
under my finger.

Absinthe

after the painting by Degas

Soon they'll drain their glasses
and walk, empty-handed
down the street,

her feet swelling
in silver, high-heeled shoes
she insists on wearing

because it's Christmas
and someone who remembers
might step out from the crowd

of late-night shoppers
and embrace them.
It's better than staying at home,

she says to herself
and sometimes murmurs
the lost child's name,

but he's listening to shadows
in the mirror
behind their heads

as they drain
their glasses
and slip into the crowd.

Aftermath

i Manequin

Stripped
by the bomb blast,
his perfect limbs
and torso
marbled with light

he could be Adonis
in summer sun
except his stone eyes
cannot see

the bouquet
where she paused
for a moment
and set it in glass.

ii Street-scape

The street
is a vagrant woman
crouching
against shop-fronts
puckered like cardboard.

Nimble as ants
policemen side-step
her entrails
coiled under stones
that spill
from cavities.

She covers her face
with soiled smoke
of hair
smouldering
under the black eye
of a lamp-post.

Intersection

Someday you'll glance in your plastic framed mirror
bought at the convenience store

near the intersection
between 6th street and the Common

and see a man looking for something
he knows he has lost –

a quiver in the furthest corner of the room –
optical illusion, or an indoors draught of air –

will bring it back. A twist of hair, brushed sideways,
slipping into its own place.

Lifeline

Two water-lines on my windscreen,
each ending in a drop
as they slip down the glass.

One, slightly ahead, evaporates.
The other settles
on a wrinkle of dust.

Traffic flow diverts me.
When I look again the drop has gone
though a smudge remains.

I think of your eyes
that time I saw you weeping.
One tear faltered, and fell.

The other steadied,
dried into your skin.

Masks

Sometimes, when I look at you,
across a table, or in a crowd,
you're wearing a mask
taut as stretched skin.

The first time, repelled,
I tore at it, dug in my fingers
until you bled,
but you had made it well,
it was tear-resistant.

Now it has grown on me
like a familiar face.
When you take it off
I turn my eyes away,

feel my skin tighten
into its own mask.

After you leave

On a road off the motorway
I drive with headlights dimmed
the way you taught me, click, down,

all it takes, simple really, one moment
full on, then click, then

a street at midnight, only
homeless footsteps; I abandon the car,
lights dying

the most noiseless way,
not even the hiss of a candle when

a hall door swings; I press my ear
to the space between swings, the unlit
air, breath I follow

Moon-milk

Love, come no closer to me than the moon
in that black cat's eye – I relish it
all the more through glass, the sheen
of its slippery falling-away
though not quite falling away –

or no closer than the cat –
a stranger to this place,
however much he rolls on his back
begging a tickle from stars –

but close as the rain-pool
his deft paws avoid
that seeps through a crack in my door,
glowing on floorboards, and warm
for this hour of the evening –
a cat's eye for all the world.

*

When I see your face appear
even the cat quivers – is he laughing
or shaking snow from his fur –
and now that I have him in my eye
how on earth did he squeeze his way here?

Undeterred, you make a spout of your hand -
or a miniature jug -
glazed where your knuckles curve
into hollows of skin – there

let me curl while you pour out the moon.

Rain Kiss

Your sister is coming down the stairs
still hiding her hair in a sixties bun.
Nothing passes between us,

only a half-heard greeting, a shadow-stare
decades old as she goes on her way
to Bridge and tea.

I detach from companions who murmur,
it's getting late –

so late at your house where we lingered
they've boarded windows and doors,
the sleepers upstairs,

and the curtain that caused all that trouble -

love, look at it one more time -
at that side-face turning away.
Turn from the hall-door, don't hurry inside,

rain-dust is softer than rain.

Pink Satin Dress

Earlier, I scrubbed my skin to bone –

it chills when dance-light dims
and your fingers caress

my best friend's spine. Silk thread
unravels at the hem –

a trail of dust slipping into crevices.
If I could hold it in my arms –

too long, too loose,
assembled in haste –

I'd stroke the hemline
snagged on glass,

transparent as your eyes
avoiding mine,

that leaves stripped bone
washed up on a shore. Look,

my pink dress shivers on stone.

Loving You

That last year we met in the café
after school – convent girls, college boys,
and Elvis on the juke-box. *Heartbreak Hotel,*
coffee, club-milks and *Hamlet.* Was he
or wasn't he? Mad. I was mad for you
in your black blazer. I somersaulted
when your knees pressed mine.

Child of Mary, framed on the mantelpiece.
Virgin. A blue ribbon around my neck.
Night prayers on the cold lino.
A hot-water bottle between my legs.
Darling. I gave you the word
from the last page of Mills and Boon,
conceived in exquisite sin.

Outside The Savoy, a long queue
humming down the street as far as
The Blue Lagoon. *G.I.Blues.* Elvis was
transformed. I saw you looking
at my best friend. Cliché - the best
days of your life. Describe it –
my mouth open, like a wound, in tears.

September Snowman

I'm rushing out the door when you shout
from the garden, still in your pyjamas,
half the contents of a burst sack -
envelopes, paper, scrunched plastic bags,
all white at a glance like patches
of leftover snow - settling on grass,
shrub and oil tank. Or is it
your hair (white at this hour
though indoors a gentler grey)
changes all to its own shade? Fragments
near a geranium stay with me
when I close the door -
- no sign of bird or cat -
like throwaway words that lodge
in unseen places, say, the heart
or a garden behind neat suburban walls.

Image

Gertrude named the willow
mirrored in the stream,

and its hoar leaves on the sliver
that split with the weight
of Ophelia's wildflowers;

but all we know is the colour
of our tree – the blossoms of course
that are only temporary.

You ask for a photograph –
a request that takes you
further away.

But I will send it –
not lake water for the grey street,
but the unnamed, growing outside,

to hold in your fingers
before it reverts to being just a tree.

Balancing Act

Laughing at my effort to lift the axe,
you steady your feet, and slowly swing

until veins, skin and muscle convulse
in stubborn rope-roots, the fightback

of old stones and earth. You heave the axe upwards
for one last strike

which requires me to steady our ancient shrub
like a giant hedgehog in my arms.

But before the downswing,
it gives, all at once,

as if to reward me for holding on
and easing it out of life.

The pickaxe slumps
in a groundswell of dust. I offer iced water,

quenching a laugh
at your effort to lift the glass.

The Broken Tree

From the base of this shadowy uphill path
its prostrate trunk seems continuous and whole,

but draw your breath on level ground
and enter the clearing around it;

borrow a child, and holding his hand
let him walk its length as far as the breach

you must lift him across,
hear him call it

the broken tree. Knots on the bark
are words withheld

when we're face to face
like the severed halves of this ancient elm

enduring the dark between us.

Oak

That I'm female is not in doubt
when each one takes his turn on the box

two hundred yards from the dead-
centre point where I frustrate

his dream of stroking an eagle to the cup.
*Only a mother could...Bitch...*are cues

to Saturday morning's dismembering.

Like a villain, tied to a stake,
I hear all my pretty birds fall from arms

that cannot withstand the thump
of a miss-hit shot.

*

Half-way to flag and end of play
three women finger what's left on my stumps

in a strip-tease wind; vowels slip
through a mesh of green as they struggle

to recall my name. One says
I should write a poem of myself

when rain draws her close to me;

the groundsman rakes branches
and feathers at my base

as if he's stroking creases on my skin
and not the deadwood I'll become.

To a Crow on a Winter Tree

Abandon that jittery business
with your tail, it makes no sense
on a bare branch....get an inkling
of what I've in mind for you –
it supersedes my first instinct
to sketch you as a makeshift
robin on a Christmas card,
especially as I have no red
marker. Don't ask me how –

it will be painless –
a kiss of sorts –
and I will lay you out
on white greaseproof paper.

Don't jump
to conclusions. Long hours staring
out the kitchen window
have not made me
heartless. Your flesh will shimmer
on a fine dust
of flour, studded with herbs,
and I will cool
white wine in a bucket of ice.

Abandon that jittery business
with your tail. It makes no sense
on a bare branch...

Nureyev's Bird Prepares to Serve

Our opponent's eyes
are fixed stars
guarding the net.
Partner, I digress,

but above the floodlights
the moon's tipsy
as a swan
in school ballet.

Now readiness
is all you ask of me,
and I'm no slave
to yesteryear –

that rattle
is only my bird-
breath tuning up
for our pas de deux.

Going for Gold

Hard to look at either face –
the winner's contorted,
pummelled,
red,
the loser's skin-stripped,
chill –

better to turn away –

a girl is dressing
in the glare,
she's running
through a tunnel of eyes,
tongue-tied,
on buckled legs.

Golf Ball in Water

It's an arm's length down,
resting on stones,
a replica of the October sun.

My daughter peers over the edge -
a pearl fisher
searching.

We take turns with the yellow rake.
The water muddies.
Let it settle and clear, she says.

But the sky, upsidedown
in the pond,
is brimming with cloud.

It's too late to roll up my sleeve,
even if my fingers could
prise the ball

from suck of mud and stone.
Cloud erases
my child in water,

erases the sun.

Inch Strand on Easter Sunday

Dust covers
lift off the strand

children unwind
kite-strings

unruffled
a jet crosses

impossible
from that height

to see the dead dog
becoming

an old rug
or the light bulb

wedged
in a footprint

like a giant tear.

Elephant in Indianapolis

We live like inmates
for a year
at *Orchard Downs*
where cornfields
not apples
hem us in
and the small print
under the sign

Apartments for Married Students.

Let loose for a day trip
to the zoo
the children dodge
my camera.
Darkly
she enters
the frame,

shuffles round
and round
on a circle
scored with sweat
from her feet,
grazing the cage
with her old-woman's hide

as if she is half asleep.

But now as I see her
through other lens,
her head still
sloping
to the ground,
she's moving in time
to the beat of a drum

like one who has lost her mind.

At Dove Cottage

Uneven as tombstones, we circle the Voice
of our guide in the miniature room –
she's diminutive too, and dressed like a latter-day nun.

Sun is forgotten on flagstone and hearth –
how on earth did they live in this place? We follow her
anecdotes up the dark stair.

Hair of the poet – here – behind glass. Thankfully
out of reach – though no doubt there's one in the group
who'd like to – well – stroke it. Once.

*Months in the winter seemed longer than years
and candles were dearer than meat.* I fear
she has singled me out. Her eyes –

surprisingly grey – land on mine, so to speak,
and see into the life of things – my longing
for air and a Grasmere cream tea.

Keepsakes

i

They fade to the colour of Marietta
biscuits offered to a child peering out
of an old woman's eyes.

That leaf, concealed in a birthday card,
shrivels to skin-tone, the shade
of summer melting on the last bus home

as a pebble warms in the deepest
cotton pocket, sheds sand in stitching
never washed out, recovers ocean

bareness lost on the shore. Unfaithful
fingers toss it with baubles and buttons,
off-white at the back of a drawer.

ii

It was unexpected. You, lingering
in the doorway, watching

until my car moved out of sight.
Perhaps that patch of sky, flittering

like a sheet washed too many times
offered you a glimpse

of our seaside bus
disappearing from childhood's kerb.

Don Cockburn, Newsreader, Speaks Again.

He steadies his bicycle against the pavilion,
unaware of my ear twisting a dial
when someone greets him with a name
that belongs to childhood's litany -
Cuchulainn, Jesus, Pearse.
Clatter of racquet, pitch of ball fades

as street sound faded when she held
a finger to her lips, lowered her head
towards uncut bread, and he entered
like one well used to that room,
her chair by the wireless,
hand spread on cloth that dared not stir

when Cockburn spoke. No one knocked
on the hall door then, tapped glass
or sat on the window sill
as Denny's workers often did,
overspill from their buckets staining our path.
My absent father looked down

from his photograph, further away
when naming began. Korea, Hong Kong, Sudan.
She stared through the window
at the long table of Ben Bulben,
as if she could see those places
etched on its darkness. Now his voice

becomes that of an ordinary man
unclipping a racquet from his bicycle,
checking string; words light as the breeze
that lifts the net. It settles again,
seems taut as it stretches from end
to end. I turn back the dial.

The Hired Car

It is ours for two whole weeks,
the black, squat weight of it
parked on the street. Ritual

newspaper under his knees,
twists of the crank, shuddering
rumble, flung-open doors,

roads off the beaten track
all to ourselves, salt-water
flesh of the mussels spat out,

lemonade in the snug.
Revving up again, never an end
to his woodbines

smoked in the dark.
His arm on her shoulder,
incline of her head,

our eyes almost closed.
Wearied out, it winds down.
In the morning, a space

where it rested, blocking
our everyday view
of the mountain,

the river, the long line
of gulls undisturbed
on the stones. No sound

of his voice. In the hall
The Independent lies
folded on the mat.

Bottom Drawer

The wardrobe
is not her own
entirely.

Across the top
forgotten, lost things
linger.

The door is loose
from too much
opening.

Inside, a space
for hide and seek,
familiar, warm.

The bottom drawer
sags with sheets
and pillowcases.

Underneath them,
silk, ivory-coloured
nightdresses,

unscented,
delicate.

An Old Man Explains...

I came in
to shelter from rain
and strayed
into *Lingerie* –

it's familiar
as the drawer
in our bedroom
full of her things

that I like to arrange
into bundles
according to shade
and sometimes

make pot-pourri –
take them out,
put in,
it fills the whole day -

let me bury
my face
in pastels,
close my eyes –

this one in my fingers
is second-skin –
like hers
before she died.

Bless me, Father…

i Absolution

Deft swipe of a plastic knob
across a child's scribble-board
and all her grotesque shapes are gone,
the way my bones drain
to the colour of a dove
when his fingers snap the grille.

*

Arches, pillars, aisles,
cubicles dissolve like Friday evenings.
Pavements twisting
down to the river
near the little street
where my home waits,
are thin underfoot, and clean.

Gulls have been busy,
and now they sleep,
belly-full with whitest crusts,
their breath is all I hear
from the rooftop of morning,
cooling my wings.

ii Atonement

Some things got under your skin –
river sludge and dead white
gulls, the texture of wool,
and my giggles disrupting
the six o'clock news.

*

Now our stretch of the river
grows older every year,
like the threadbare hat
you wore in the cold –
and almost wore out.
I gave it to you. Remember?

The unwrapping was easy.
Paper on the floor,
our hands touching
the double-knit edge.
You slipped the hat
over your ears –

warm as honey, you said –
the darker wool
fitted your head
as if it had grown on you
all the time I stood there praying.

Naming Them

The back of his children's heads never stir
when he returns from a day spent
alone, five miles from the town, at Glencar
waterfall in rain showers. 'Shoo', he hisses
at Gordon the cat asleep in his armchair,
longing to kick him to kingdom-come
while they kneel with their mother, chanting
the Rosary. 'Jesus wept', is all he can mutter

as he drinks his dinner in Mulligan's snug
and hears the youngest knock on the window.
Or is it the eldest? Or one of the two
in between? Peas in a pod, crouched
over schoolbooks. 'They're teaching you nothing
in that place. I can name every blossom
I touched today – hawthorn, catmint,
woodbine, wild woodbine. Listen!'

'Let's go for a walk to the Orchard...'

Who will notice she's no longer
following as we pass

the Custom House
flattened by a new road,

the low wall running
alongside a river we thought was the sea,

then the mountain
concealed on days like this

by a veil of cloud,
spread, like her shadow,

on blue space,
distance never decreasing?

PART 2

At Brittas Bay
for Ben, June 2005

Fold this white day,
edge to edge,

lose no thread
in the sand,

along an inner seam
let the loved child

skip over waves
you swing for him.

Snowdrop in November
for Katie Louise, 30-11-04

Flush of light on the patch where I'd scattered
a promise of bulbs

not expecting this early peel-back of dusk,
like a bride's hand lifting the veil from her face,

or that glimpse through the half-open door
of mittens and wrap-over vests on a bedspread

lit by a street-lamp - white petal-folds
and you, close by,

listening to your mother, her heartbeat's
caress on the unborn curve of your head.

You Have a   Son

chant all the voices, or one voice
or mouth in the cave
of a sea-song
you float back to sleep in,
to wake in the room
where your waters broke,
splatters like birthmarks
on a stranger's face

that shrinks as it stirs into focus.
You finger his skin
with an eye on the door,
like a visitor to a gallery
who flouts the warning signs,
until a bell vibrates,
and you shudder under the weight
of a hand on your shoulder,

before the step-back begins
and milestones slip past
as if they're happening
in sleep to a stranger
who wears your face
and listens to a voice
in the cave of memory
telling you, he is your   son.

Fishing with Ben, Aged Four

I'm cutting a fish: not cod
frozen in breadcrumbs, or a fillet
of salmon with a day to go
before its sell-by date, this
is a scorpionfish, breathless
colour you wouldn't dream of naming.

It doesn't flinch
when I thread a needle
and pierce its jaw forever open
in a yawn that could start
a whole room yawning, even you
standing on tip-toe, ready

for the swim of your life
with a fish tied to the finger you plunge
through kitchen and hall,
flooded with Caribbean water
I didn't cut from pages
of *National Geographic*.

Choreographer, Aged Two

Eight jigsaw pieces, all shades
of a blue girl on the verge
of dancing, the exact blue

on the box you push to one side,
for you have no need of pictures,
you follow the colour of finger-tips,

swivelling arms and legs
until your girl's a Picasso
dancing on the verge of blue.

He Writes the Alphabet Backwards

His vision of Apple is green on white,
perfectly formed, as if it never grew from seed,

is simply there, like the first sound of a story
he knows by heart.

He'll reach it by scattering white dust – a list
on his mother's kitchen blackboard –

spaghetti, tea-bags, frozen peas – his journey lit
by a Giraffe's eye

watching his spiral of letters
weave their way to the highest branch.

Here he is, chanting his song,
all the way back to a Zebra's smile.

The Bullies

wait on the far side, grinning
with teeth-white eyes. The lollypop woman
stretches her arms out, but your feet
stick

like porridge. Your mother is rinsing
breakfast bowls. Her woolly sleeves
rolled up to her elbows. Mother bear,
and baby...

cry baby bear, your new name.
Cars strain like racehorses waiting
for the gun. The crack of the whip.
You remember

the tightrope walker, tiny above
the roars. Head high. Eyes in his feet.
Cats' eyes, tom cats, grinning.
You are a tight rope walker,

your feet sweat on the rope...

Why Doesn't She Cry?

The Girl in Pink who couldn't stop Smiling
falls on floorboards. You're almost asleep,
and now that I'm half-way down the stairs
it's too late to replace the book on your shelf.

Tonight its covers - open at the spine,
and warmed by your teddy-bear lamp –
are a tent for the girl
who never gets cross with questions

you keep on asking – why the moon is round,
or why stars fall. But Katie, here's the thing –
now you're asleep, I'm watching Sky News
and seeing your face leaves me bereft

of every word but beautiful –
it's dark outside, but soon you'll forget
the *Girl in Pink* folding her tent,
or why she's gone.

Lighting the Tree in Greystones Plaza

It's mid-November, and grey-stone water
chatters like old women's bones in the ocean
you can almost see from the watch-out of
your grandfather's shoulders; sorrow
(a big word, I know) light as a fish bone
or the tooth print of that robin picking
bread in your garden, is as far from this
newly-built Plaza as our child-eyes seeing

a journey that began in the bicycle shop window
with Santy - that's what we called him – peddling
a racer that suited him down to the ground;
the great tree flares, and Santa dismounts from
his Rover - of course you can't see it -
the handlebars are black, and slippery as sea-stones.

Child on a Small Landing

Sometimes she returns
to the top of the stairs

like a shadow-spool,
cradling her knees,

her breath indrawn
on a cobweb of words

that betrays all she's heard
about time. Voices,

through the half-open
door below,

still sharpen like needles
on her name –

her name
stripped

to a bone-
spool that trembles

on the small landing.

Offering up the Child

Where candles float in bowls
she's led by the hand –

Tumbelina, sucking her thumb –
dipped in one

washing warm breath
up to her chin,

submerged in liquid love
she'll struggle all her life

to siphon from toenails,
from cracks in her skin.

New Things

She's no intention of falling asleep,
but new laced boots beside the pillow

stand on guard as her fingers loosen.
Outside the abattoir's closed gate

straw lines the floor of morning trucks.
She dreams the sky isn't a ceiling

and somewhere a woman's footsteps fade.
Thin heels soft as a lamb's heart beating.

Sandcastle

A handful of windows, misshapen like shells,
slip though your fingers

when I scoop clumps of shoreline sand
and pebbles like eyes disappear.

What can I tell you about your blue plastic shovel
buckled at the rim,

about windows that hide things
though we squint till it hurts,

about walls that crumble when your back is turned -
what can I tell you about the sea?

Of Bells and Apple Trees

In full flight, I revel in yesterday's orchards,
rolling my tongue over slivers lodged in my teeth,

tossing a windfall towards faces with no flicker back
when I ask if they've ever gone apple-picking.

Only three out of thirty hands in air,
so how can I seduce them

with Frost's apple trees, or the scent
of barrels waiting to be filled

now they're already half-way to sleep
the final bell's echo fermenting their dreams?

Songs of a Doomed School

When dust settles,
and my corridors, blackboards
broken blinds
cling to a workman's boot,

he'll rinse children's voices
under a tap. Listen
to the swell
of a blue choir singing.

*

Straggler,
don't you know

my last bell
has gone

and the spidery
name

you carved
on a desk

with the date
you were born?

*

Daily, the stranger grows
in my playing field,
already she's twice my height,

but light,
like a child's smile,
filters through all her crevices;

her roots are embedded
in uncut grass
that barely smothers

giggles and smoke-rings
from Rosie,
and all of her mates.

*

Hollow as the shell
of an ocean-liner,
or the carcass of a whale

sheltering air, I'm open
to bone-pickers for a week.

What can I offer
when they search
for souvenirs -

the ghost of a teacher
shaking chalk dust from her hair?

*

Somedays, I hold
what breath I've left
and listen to the tune
of the new building –

steel entering stone –

until the tallest girl
dulls the chorus
with an ancient window-pole.

Reviewing the Syllabus

i Sailing to Byzantium with Mr Yeats

Years ago, in the classroom, I set him off
on his voyage, watching with my students
from the far side of a shore, his stick arms
protruding from the tatters of his coat,
and all of us were young birds
keeping a distance while he took
forty minutes to sail out of our lives
and spread new wings on a metal tree.

All's changed, he murmurs now in my ear
while they avert their eyes and long
for the bell to disgorge them into corridors
of flesh, before I step into the boat
with a scarecrow who claps his hands
and sings like a maniac.

ii Ophelia's Ghost

She's almost invisible, pale,
of course – you always struggle
with her name and the odd way
she resurfaces at term's end
stirring your conscience. Typically
she settles anywhere, often
at the back of the class,
sometimes in the middle,
once, in the front row
beside that pair driving you
mad with questions: which lines
should they learn by heart, and why
did no one help the drowning girl?

iii Unseen Poem

Steady now,
whispers, giggles
subside,

distribute A4 sheets,
white windows
on teak,

watch eyes
blending song-
colour that spills

from the bowl
cupped
in your hands.

iv The Stand Alone Text

Start with that beech on the road to Sligo,
solitary, there, as if all other trees
shrivelled like pebbles at Ben Bulben's base,

pause in the gateway opposite
leaf and shade you'd be lost without,

sing (yes, they'll laugh), then
louder sing of the bird
who keeps the high branch for himself.

Last Year's Shade

Someone forgot to close the window –
no one noticed Jamie's poem, missing
from the back wall of second-years
'secret garden' poems. Here, on the top floor,
I hear footsteps on gravel below.

On the wall, a square of yellow brick
announces it's time to clear the rest –
white is last year's shade. They leave
in threes and twos - and one

always alone – if she stays behind
no one will notice. I'm closing the door
for the last time – clearing gravel
from the unseen lines of a poem.

iii Garden of the Missing

We stayed so long
in the domed tree-house, roofed

with armfuls of leaves we plugged
into skyholes over our heads, air-borne voices

were thin as a sleepy bird's song
or the scraping of laurels

sculptured in stone. Names
scribbled on fragments of paper,

or fingered in sand before we were born,
all they have for calling us home.

iv Bones of Sand

Only a handful of years
between the onset of his sleeping here

and the barefoot hour of castles and sandboats,
between the stroking of hair on a chin

he wanted to bristle like gorse
and a child's face

smooth as the marble cross
where I rest my fingers now,

seeing an old man retreat from sun,
his profile invisible as a sandman's bones.

v Close to the Pointe du Hoc

Side by side, on towels unfurled
like shrouds from a rainbow,

our dead weight bodies
that can climb no more,

even for a glimpse of the ruined battery,
endure thistle and thorn,

but not the disturbed
quiver of ants

heaving like a black shape
cut loose on the shore.

vi Low Tide at Port en Bessin

This evening, no ice-packed marbled catch,
clinging to seaweed and rock

only shellfish discoloured as bone,
and parents who squint at

small hands dangling
fishnets of clink and spill;

row-boats slither in mud like tipsy old men
who can't tell why they're here

with children between them
and shell-song echoing.

vii Procession at St. Laurent

On waste ground, no struggle
for car-space. Orderly lines retreat

from *Overflow Closed*
to arms-length rest beside doors eased open

on unguarded grass we're free
to traverse, their colour metallic

as sea-glaze in sun; a procession
following an anthem of waves,

wing-curve and stretch
of a seagull's throat.

viii Apples and Pearls

Voices call our names
but we're safe in the garden

we entered this morning, with children
who crouch between bramble and hedge

offering apples through a gap
made for hands and pennies.

You'll find us if you listen
for a shiver of leaves

and copper lightening
to mother-of-pearl.

ix Some link arms,

baseball caps switched back to front,
combats at half-mast,

and t-shirts noisy
with words they can't speak –

like children who seem to have grown
in sleep, they weave down side paths of

cypress and pine, close to long lines
of names - Chuck, Jamie and all

those white arms
linked in the distance.

x Veteran Revisits the Pointe du Hoc

On the tightrope
of his family's frozen breath,

clinging to their eyes
as far as he dares, he belly-slides

down vertical gorse, to the limit
of his grandson's cry – a show-stopper

drowning the sea-fall of stones -
it vibrates on a line tight as gut,

familiar as gull-song he cradled all that night,
with both hands he grasps it close to his chest.